Woodturning
Masterclass

Woodturning
Masterclass
Artistry · Style · Inspiration

Tony Boase

GUILD OF MASTER CRAFTSMAN PUBLICATIONS LTD

First published 1995 by
Guild of Master Craftsman Publications Ltd,
166 High Street, Lewes,
East Sussex BN7 1XU

© Tony Boase 1995

ISBN 0 946819 84 X

Designed by Teresa Dearlove

Typeface: Gill

Printed in Hong Kong by H & Y Printing Ltd

Contents

To Jacky, Petra and Marc for their support while I was 'Turning Mad'.

Acknowledgements

I wish to thank the following who in one way or another helped make this book happen: Liz Inman at Guild of Master Craftsman Publications for her encouragement, and for keeping me at it when I was running out of steam; Alex Woolf for help with the editing; Teresa Dearlove for the design; Nicola Bealing, Pod Clare, Wilma Kaye, Carol White, Ann Firmager, Liz O'Donnell, and Helen and Michael Williams for their hospitality while I was on the road. Thanks also to Lionel Bromberg for help with my turning and to Jim-Lad Sugden for accompanying me on burr hunting forays.

Introduction

Although photography has been the means by which I have earned my living for the past 25 years, woodturning has been a passion of mine for even longer. What better way could there be, I thought, of combining the two than to write a book on the subject?

My aim was to produce a portrait, in words and photographs, of each of a dozen distinguished turners. The book would show them at work, describe why they began turning, and include examples of their best work.

I set off in January 1994 on a journey that would take me the length and breadth of the British Isles, visiting the turners in their workshops, photographing them and staying up till the early hours talking shop. Wherever I went I was met with generous hospitality and if there is one thing I have learnt over the past year it is that turners are a decent bunch! My thanks to the 12 for their time, cooperation, and patience.

For this book I have concentrated on turners specializing in bowls, hollow forms and sculptural turning. While I admire the skills involved in other types of woodturning, my preference is for the faceplate and this is where my interest lies. Any selection is bound to be subjective, but I feel that the 12 turners who appear here are a fair representation of the high standard of work being produced in Britain today. I hope that those who for logistical reasons I was not able to include this time around will agree to appear in Volume Two, upon which I intend to embark next year.

Although there are numerous tips to be gleaned from studying the workshop photographs, I never intended this book to be another instruction manual. I decided on more of a reportage approach and hope that the resulting photographs will give a different perspective to the art of the turner.

It has been pointed out to me that in the majority of photographs in this book the turners are working without adequate face and lung protection. This was a deliberate ploy. I decided that as page after page of helmeted heads would make for very dull pictures, it would benefit the book to ask those taking part to appear without this essential safety aid. They reluctantly agreed, as, without exception, all are very aware of the dangers inherent in woodturning and always work with full face and lung protection – and so should you!

My own interest in turning goes back to my childhood in East Africa where my father worked as an eye surgeon. I recall him spending almost as much time in his workshop as he did in the operating theatre. He taught me how to turn and on his death in 1986, I inherited his lathe and have been ' turning mad' ever since.

For the technically minded, the workshop photographs were taken with a Nikon F4 using a variety of lenses from 35mm to 200mm. The still-life studio photographs were taken with a Rollei 6006 with a 150mm lens and a Nikon F4 with a 105mm macro lens. Lighting throughout was by Broncolour. I used Fuji RDP100 film, processed by T & S Lightbox in London and Streamline Colour in Cambridge.

anthony bryant

A walk along the narrow lanes above Porthleven is not without its dangers. Keep an eye open for an intrepid cyclist in full racing kit careering around the next bend at the speed of light. Blink, and you will have missed Anthony Bryant, taking time off from his lathe to clear his lungs with his daily 40 mile sprint along the Cornish coast.

Born in Cornwall, the son of a builder and carpenter, he cut his teeth on a treadle lathe before graduating to a Myford. On leaving school he went into banking and it was while working his way up the ladder – bored out of his mind – that an advertisement for a turning course with Mike Law caught his eye. He enrolled and before long Mike became his friend and mentor. As an adept student he was soon helping Mike instruct others on the course. By now, turning was taking up all his spare time and it became clear that he would have to choose between the bank and the lathe. No contest; the lathe won and in 1983 he became a full-time turner.

Anthony Bryant is known the world over for his extraordinarily thin, wet-turned vessels. That he creates these with minimal equipment – a couple of specially ground gouges and a reconditioned Dominion lathe rescued from a naval dockyard; not a scraper or fancy tool in sight – is even more remarkable. By turning thin, much of the stress inherent in unseasoned wood, invariably leading to splits and shakes, is removed. The seasoning, and what happens to the piece while this is taking place, is an integral part of the process.

His distinctive style has evolved naturally through trial and error. Influences are more likely to have come from friends who are potters rather than other turners. 'Apart from Mike Law I've not seen other turners at work so I don't know how they do it. I just do what I do.' It is this singular approach which makes Anthony's work unique, aided by a continual refinement of technique and a finely tuned sense of form and balance. He sets himself very high standards and does not hesitate to put through the bandsaw work that most turners would be proud of.

Among his peers Anthony remains something of an enigma. His secluded existence in deepest Cornwall and his avoidance of the demonstration/symposium circuit has led to him being accused of being aloof, even arrogant. It was therefore with some trepidation that I set off to Cornwall to spend a couple of days photographing him for this book. I was in for a pleasant surprise. Serious about his work without taking himself too seriously would be a fair description.

Anthony sells his work through fine art galleries in the UK and elsewhere. America is proving receptive and Japan has begun to show interest. Both the Victoria & Albert Museum and the Crafts Council have his pieces in their collections.

Where to now? Talking with him I got the impression that he is looking beyond the restrictions imposed by the lathe. A move into pure sculpture could be on the cards. Whichever direction he chooses, the results are sure to be interesting. If all else fails he could always get on his bike.

My initial reaction when I saw the huge piece of brown oak that Anthony had selected to turn was, 'you'll never get that on your lathe'. I was soon proved wrong.

Opposite
The selected brown oak log is halved with the chainsaw.

Top
The profile is roughly shaped with the chainsaw to reduce the weight prior to attaching it to the faceplate.

Left and below
Mounted on the Dominion lathe, the outside is shaped and the base trued to take the faceplate.

Top
Back outside, the core is removed – and saved for further use – by plunge cutting with the chainsaw. This is a highly skilled operation and not recommended for the uninitiated.

Left
The core is gently eased out with a crowbar.

Top right
With the piece reversed on to the lathe and the profile now shaped, it is dried with a hot air gun to make it easier to sand.

Centre right
The inside is removed to an overall thickness of ⅛in (3mm).

Bottom right
Frequent visits to the sharpening wheel are essential for keeping the tool razor sharp.

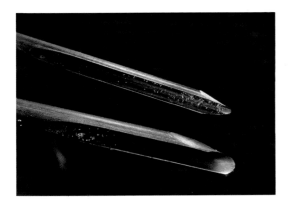

Top
These two specially ground gouges are used for 98 per cent of the turning.

Above
The tool rack.

Right
Off the lathe the completed piece will be hand sanded, treated with tung oil and allowed to dry in a cool room to acquire its final shape.

Brown oak
(see pages 4–9)
W: 24in (610mm)

Brown oak
H: 20in (508mm)

Burr oak
H: 24in (610mm)
W: 20in (508mm)

Brown oak
H: 24in (610mm)

paul clare

After leaving school at 15, and a short spell in a hair clipper factory, Paul was indentured as an apprentice sheet metal worker with London Transport. This was to last for five years plus one year as an 'improver'. To hear him describe the workmanship that went into producing the old RT London bus it's no wonder that they are to be found 35 years later trundling the roads of Bangladesh. Laid off in the 1960s for poor timekeeping – 'I might have been late but my work was always completed on time and never sent back to be redone' – Paul still finds it hard to greet the dawn, and family and friends have learnt to stay well clear until he's had at least three mugs of sweet, strong coffee.

He was soon back in employment as a workshop technician at the local grammar school, and from here he moved to the 3D workshops at Hornsea College of Art where he met his wife, Pod. In 1972, tired of London, they moved to Wales and started an antique and restoration business. Lathe skills built up over the years came in handy and soon began to take over; by 1987 Paul was turning full time.

Prior to my visiting Paul at his workshop on a hill overlooking the sea at Aberath, I was mainly aware of his split-burr vessels. However, I came away convinced that here was one of the most accomplished turners at work anywhere today. He is as capable of producing simple salad bowls as the idiosyncratic gallery pieces he is known for. Inspiration can come from fungi, old farm machinery and by generally keeping his eyes open. A punk rocker's hairdo gave him the idea for one piece he showed me. Working mainly in burrs, he incorporates techniques picked up over the years in the metalwork and restoration business. A lot of his work involves surface texturing using metalworking tools, carving, sand blasting, scorching, pickling and microwaving. He has a cavalier approach to the finer points of turning technique. When I asked him what microwave setting he intended giving the split burr piece I had just watched him turn, he replied, 'I'll try it on fish and if that doesn't work I'll give it five minutes on beef.'

It was at Loughborough '91 that Paul received the long overdue recognition of his peers. He arrived clutching a carrier bag containing a few examples of his work and it took some effort on the part of the then AWGB chairman Tony Waddilove to persuade him to display them in the Instant Gallery. They were an immediate success and without doubt one of the highlights of the show. His new found fame, with turners beating a path to his door, has come as a bit of a shock to the system. Invitations to demonstrate come from far and wide, however, as he hates travelling and can't stand flying, most are declined. This is a pity as he is a natural demonstrator who deserves a larger audience.

The bulk of his work is turned on a modified Cincinnati lathe weighing in at over two tons. Apart from extra-long gouges made specially for him by Henry Taylor, he makes most of his own tools including a heavy-duty version of the Stewart system – the original was just not up to the punishment Paul dealt out while turning. He is pretty scathing about a lot of the accessories that are being mass produced for the market today, with the exception of his Axminster four-jaw which he would not be without. He can't take seriously chucks held together by rubber bands – 'what kind of engineering do you call that?'

Away from his lathe Paul can be found tending his vegetables in his rabbit-proof garden, or teaching his parrots a few choice phrases from his south London vocabulary.

I asked Paul to turn one of his famous split pots and accompanied him to a field behind his workshop where he selected a suitable piece of burr oak from a pile exposed to the elements.

Top
Selecting a suitable log of burr oak from the woodpile.

Centre
Converting the rough burr into a cylinder with a chainsaw.

Bottom
Mounted between centres on the Cincinnati lathe, the piece is turned true using a ½in (13mm) gouge.

paul clare

Top
A metalworker's knurling tool is used to texture the surface.

Centre
Paul's selection of tools.

Bottom
Removing the core using a Forstner bit mounted in the headstock.

Opposite top
Rough shaping with a ½in (13mm) gouge.

Opposite bottom
A parting tool is used to make the grooves.

Top right
Once the grooves are finished the piece is reversed on to the lathe with an internal jam-fit chuck.

Centre right
The base is detailed, turned off and. . .

Bottom right
. . . cleaned up with a chisel.

Top
The complete piece prior to being . . .

Centre
. . . dunked in a bucket of ferrous oxide.

Below
It is given a good hose down before . . .

Opposite
. . . microwaving to encourage movement.

Burr oak split pot
(see pages 16–21)
H: 8in (203mm)

Grass tree
H: 8in (203mm)

**Burr oak, turned
and carved
H: 12in (305mm)**

Burr oak, multi axis
D: 8in (203mm)

melyvn firmager

Melvyn discovered woodturning in 1980 while looking for a means to express the inner beauty of the wood that until then had usually ended up in his fire grate. In those days he was working in publishing while practising spiritual healing and playing pedal steel guitar in a country-and-western band in his spare time.

It was Dale Nish's books, *Creative Woodturning* and *Artistic Woodturning,* that opened his eyes to what was possible; in particular the featured work of David Ellsworth and Ed Moulthrop 'blew his mind'. In the early days he made the usual range of salad bowls, platters and goblets. Within a year he was experimenting with wet/green wood, making paper-thin vessels. He turned professional in 1986 and made his first attempts at the hollow form the following year. Right from the start he designed and made his own tools as he felt those on the market left a lot to be desired.

Melvyn feels that hollow forms – like crystals – have healing potential, the empty vessel becoming the holder of energy and creative forces represented by the womb. It seems appropriate that someone so preoccupied with the mystic should end up living in the West Country. Melvyn the woodturner producing as if by magic his hollow forms does not seem too far removed from Merlin the magician. They even look similar!

Melvyn is strongly influenced by nature, in particular fruit, seed pods, gourds and – not least – the female form. He was somewhat taken aback when I suggested that he had taken the hollow form about as far as it could go. 'Have I? I buzz with ideas all the time, some of which occasionally manifest themselves in my work. I have little sense of direction, nor see the need for one. To flow is an ideal state of being – I'm working on it'. When I visited him he was turning a series of exquisite multi-rim vessels in locally felled eucalyptus.

Melvyn divides his time between turning personal work for exhibitions and demonstrating both here and in the States where he is becoming something of a celebrity. He also runs courses in natural-edge and hollow-form turning from his workshop in Somerset. Here one learns to master his somewhat intimidating – but nevertheless user-friendly – Firmager angle tools. As most students end up buying these tools and, once they have got home, forget how to sharpen them, Melvyn has had a range of profiles manufactured in pewter to remind them of the correct bevels – a brilliant idea! If you are thinking of attending one of his courses I can readily recommend the farmhouse B & B run by his wife Ann who provides the most substantial breakfast you are likely to find anywhere in the West Country.

Melvyn sells his work through his own gallery and others in the UK as well as the del Mano in Los Angeles where, unfortunately, the 1993 earthquake damaged a number of his – uninsured – finer pieces. He was one of two UK turners whose work was selected for the international lathe-turned object show, Challenge IV.

Melvyn's workshop
is an extension of
his personality, neither
of which would seem
out of place in the
Appalachian Mountains.

**A eucalyptus blank
attached to the lathe by a
screw chuck. The lathe is
Melvyn's own variable-
speed design – a hybrid of
rudimentary engineering
and advanced electronics.**

Top left

The profile is roughly shaped by plunge cutting with Melvyn's specially ground nib gouge.

Centre left

Further shaping with the scrapy gouge.

Bottom left

Final shaping with Melvyn's multi-purpose parting tool, here used as a scraper.

Top right

Checking the profile with the lathe stopped.

Bottom right

The parting tool now comes into its own, reaching the parts other tools can't reach.

Top left
The neck is shaped prior to hollowing.

Bottom left
The rim is turned to ¹⁄₁₆in (1.5mm).

Above
The thickness is frequently checked with a pair of gynaecological forceps that Melvyn picked up on a stall in a Bristol market.

Opposite top
Hollowing.

Opposite left
Pewter models of the correct sharpening profiles of gouges available from Melvyn.

Opposite right
Close up of the Firmager angle tools used in all his hollow form work.

Eucalyptus
(see pages 28–33)
H: 10in (254mm)

Eucalyptus 'Flower'
H: 8in (203mm)

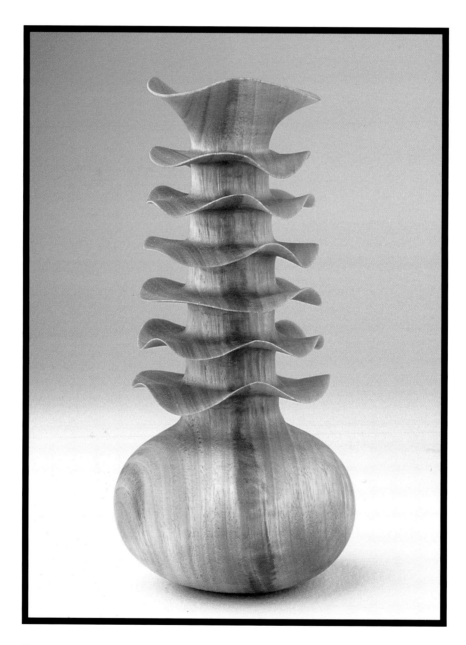

Eucalyptus, multi rim
H: 10in (254mm)

**Spalted beech, sand
blasted
H: 24in (610mm)**

tobias kaye

Tobias' first memory of a lathe was when he was ten years old hearing his father referring to an uncle's lathe as 'something on which you can make anything you like so long as it's round'. He has been fighting this assumption ever since. He came across the same lathe 12 years later when he took up a teaching post at his uncle's school.

His education at the Rudolf Steiner School in Forest Row encouraged the development of his creative skills. On leaving he travelled to Colorado for a working holiday in forestry followed by a succession of jobs including coffin maker, computer programmer, boat builder and bartender, before ending up as a care assistant at Wynestones School. It was here that he first tried his hand at turning. Tobias was helped by the fact that Cecil Jordan, who had previously taught at the school, still lived nearby and was on hand to help him master the technique. Tobias is the first to acknowledge his debt to Cecil and others who have influenced him along the way, including Del Stubbs, Giles Gilson, Hans Weissflog, Bert Marsh and Ray Key, as well as the potter, Bernard Leach. He opened his first workshop on 1 January 1982 in Stroud, moving to his present home in Devon in 1985.

From the outset Tobias made a decision not to specialize. He is just as adept at turning replacement parts for furniture restoration as he is at one-off exhibition pieces in carefully selected English hardwoods.

In 1986 he fitted a string to an acoustically formed bowl and thus began the development of the 'sounding bowl'. These have proved so popular with music therapists that there is a year's waiting list for them. He has even given a paper to the Oxford Music Conference on 'The Sounding Bowl and Music Therapy in Palliative Care'.

Tobias finds that teaching and writing are taking up more and more of his time these days to the extent that he only manages to spend about a third of his time turning. His regular column in *Practical Woodworking* about the latest trends and gizmos is always a good read. One of his teaching commitments is as visiting tutor in turning to HM Prison, Dartmoor. On one infamous occasion it was discovered to the prison officers' horror that he had innocently brought with him into the workshops a 28-inch chainsaw. All hell broke loose as visions of tabloid headlines reading 'Dartmoor Chainsaw Massacre' flashed in front of the warders' eyes! The chainsaw is now left at home.

His latest project is the launch in 1995 of a Woodturning Faculty to train professional designer/turners. He plans a one-year course with the aim of enabling students to attain the highest standards in all aspects of turning. To this end he has acquired a 2000 square foot workshop which he is equipping with all the facilities, including a photographic studio. Details of this course are available from Tobias at his Buckfastleigh workshop.

The area around Totnes in Devon is very popular with artists and craftsmen and it was partly this, and the proximity of Dartington, that prompted Tobias to set up shop on the edge of the national park at Buckfastleigh.

Top
Attaching a 6in (152mm) faceplate to the planed side of an elm burr.

Centre
Lead weights help to balance out the unevenness of the burr.

Bottom
A block of wood shaped to fit the uneven profile of the burr is attached with long screws through the bark into solid wood. The screw holes will be filled with chips of bark once the turning is complete to enable the screw chuck to be fitted and the piece reversed on to the lathe.

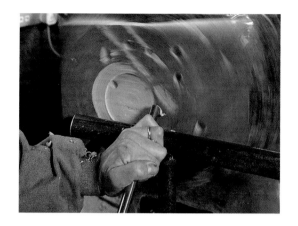

Top left
The burr is now ready for a recess to be turned into the block to take the dovetail jaws of the Axminster chuck.

Top right
With the piece reversed on to the outboard side of the lathe, the centre is removed with a ½in (13mm) bowl gouge.

Above left
The jagged profile is carefully shaped.

Above right
The recess is set off with a raised bead.

The completed turning
awaits its final sanding.

**Power sanding is carried out with
the piece revolving and stationary.**

Above
The piece is finished with a liberal coat of nutshell herbal oil.

Left
Mike the blacksmith from next door drops by for a chat.

Opposite
Stringing a sounding bowl.

Burr elm
(see pages 40–45)
W: 18in (457mm)

**Sycamore sounding
bowl
D: 14in (356mm)**

Canker-formed elm
D: 30in (762mm)

**Sycamore sounding
bowl**
D: 18in (457mm)

ray key

Ray's love affair with wood goes back to his childhood when many a happy hour was spent with carving knife and fretsaw. He came across his first lathe in his school workshop while in his teens. On leaving school he was apprenticed for five years in wood and metal pattern marking. Jobs that followed introduced him to clay and fibreglass modelling; eventually he joined Chrysler to work in their styling studio. He attributes his knowledge of design and form to his time spent with this car giant.

Along the way he married Liz and, unable to afford furniture for the marital nest, convinced her it would be a good idea to buy a lathe with their limited funds and make some himself. The dining room table made then is still in use today. As this was many years before the advent of the instructional video, it was Frank Pain's book *The Practical Woodturner*, permanently propped up beside the lathe, that taught Ray the basics. Before long, by working all hours, he was supplying craft shops in and around Coventry.

In 1965, disillusioned with industry, and encouraged and supported by Liz, he threw in the day job and became a full-time turner. They moved to Evesham where Liz opened a shop selling Ray's turning as well as pottery and jewellery from other craftspeople. Having seen from the other side how hard it is for gallery/craft shops to run at a profit, Ray can fully appreciate why they need the oft-criticized 100 per cent mark up in order to survive. His range in those days included candlesticks, platters, salt and pepper pots and little mice with leather tails and ears. Much-sought-after collector's items, these!

In 1981, Richard Raffan and Ray visited the United States. The work he observed being produced there was light years ahead of anything he had seen in the UK. Returning home he decided that the American approach was the way forward. No more bread-and-butter work – gallery pieces only. Before emigrating to Australia, Richard Raffan asked Ray if he would like to take over his contract to supply David Mellor's Kitchen Shops with salad bowls. Ray turned down this offer, preferring to concentrate on 'art' rather than 'craft'. The result was that he nearly starved and was only saved from going under by a direct approach from David Mellor with a large order for domestic items. He has never forgotten this, and today his work is divided equally between his gallery pieces – and salad bowls, platters and bread boards for the domestic market.

Ray has probably done more than anyone to put turning on the map and gain it the respect it deserves. He works tirelessly on behalf of the craft and was founding chairman of the AWGB, a post he held for four years. He is a popular figure on the lecture and demonstration circuit both in the UK and abroad. He prefers to do his teaching in the States as courses there are usually for five days, which he feels is long enough for students to really get to grips with the subject. He has written two excellent books – *Woodturning and Design* and *The Woodturner's Workbook* – and recently released three videos, directed by Dale Nish, on making boxes. He has an ongoing battle with his great friend Bert Marsh as to who makes the best box. Judge for yourself by visiting their stands at the Chelsea Crafts Fair held each autumn in the Old Town Hall.

After years of working in
a Nissen hut Ray has recently
moved into a purpose-built
workshop attached to his
house outside Evesham.
Needless to say it is
a thoroughly professional
set up.

Opposite top
**An 18in (457mm) lacewood
blank is attached to the
Graduate short-bed lathe by
using a faceplate ring.**

Opposite bottom
**The profile is worked with a
bowl gouge designed by Jerry
Glazer, using steel developed
for the space industry, and . . .**

Above
**. . . Ray's specially ground
gouges made for him by
Henry Taylor.**

Centre
**The final profile is worked
with a scraper.**

Right
Power sanding.

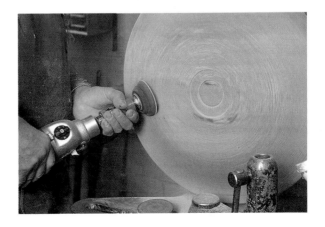

Top left
Applying a coat of liquid paraffin.

Centre left
With the piece reversed on to the lathe and held by an Axminster four-jaw chuck, the centre is removed with the Glazer gouge.

Bottom left
A final coat of liquid paraffin.

Opposite top left
Wooden jaws mounted on Ray's Moulthrop lathe.

Opposite top right
With the piece held in the wooden jaws, the chuck recess is removed . . .

Right
. . . taking great care to stay clear of the flying paddles.

Left
Rough-turned bowls are left to season for about two months before being returned to the lathe for final turning.

Top
Ray's specially ground tools.

Above
Boxes ready for the Chelsea Crafts Fair.

57

Lacewood
(see pages 52–57)
D: 20in (508mm)

Claro walnut
D: 12in (305mm)

Birch-masur
H: 3–4in (76–102mm)

Burr elm
H: 12in (305mm)

bert marsh

While researching for this piece I came across an article in an old issue of *Woodworking Today* describing Bert Marsh as the grand master of woodturning. Few would dispute this. Bert's life has been spent working with wood and, as he says, it is 'the love of it, coupled with an understanding of its way, that has influenced my work'.

He was apprenticed at 14 to a cabinetmaker in Brighton producing quality commissioned furniture that occasionally involved the use of a primitive belt-driven lathe. A part-time job teaching evening classes led to a full-time post lecturing in furniture making at Brighton Art College, and eventually, on Ernest Joyce's retirement, Bert took over the running of the furniture-making course. Despite the busy schedule, he managed to find time to keep up his turning, producing a selection of bowls that became more and more intricate as time went by. Offered a sabbatical in 1979, he decided to devote it to turning, culminating in a one-man exhibition of his work. A heart attack and subsequent open-heart surgery terminated his teaching career. Looking around for something less stressful to occupy himself with he decided on woodturning, and in 1983 he became a full-time turner.

Bert considers himself a craftsman rather than an artist. 'There are people out there calling themselves artists just because they can produce a natural-edge bowl. An awful lot of pretentious rubbish is talked and written about turning. Much of what is passed off as "art" would have been better off left on the tree!'

Bert's work has its own personality, with a strong emphasis on the non-functional. His technical expertise and knowledge of his raw material allows him to concentrate on design rather than technique. He was experimenting with scorching, texturing and colouring years before today's Young Turks made it all the rage. When his natural-edge laburnum vessels first appeared they created quite a stir – nothing like them had been seen before. Inspiration comes from keeping his eyes open, the roof line of Brighton's Royal Pavilion proving a rich source of ideas.

Although Bert doesn't teach any more – 20 years was plenty long enough – he is a frequent demonstrator at seminars and shows. He is on the register of the Worshipful Company of Turners, is a fellow of Designer Craftsmen, and an honorary member of the Guild of Master Craftsmen.

Bert is a walking testimonial to the skills of his heart surgeon. As if the prodigious output from his workshop were not enough, he keeps fit with 20 lengths of the local pool each day, though he has no plans as yet to join the hardy group who take to the sea off Brighton every day of the year.

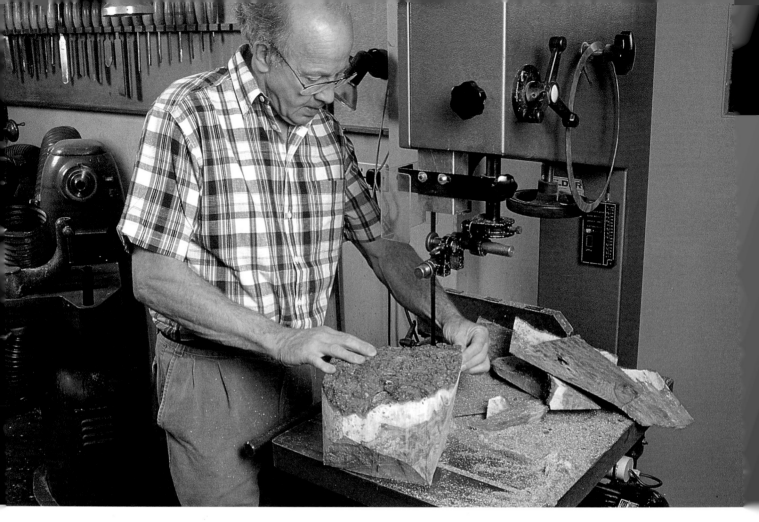

The grand master of woodturning
lives over the shop, so to speak.
The ground floor and garage
of his house, built on the side
of one of Brighton's steeper hills,
have been converted into
a workshop from where,
on a clear day, Bert can
see the sea.

Opposite top
Rough shaping the elm burr on the band saw.

Opposite centre
Mounted on a screw chuck on the Graduate lathe, the profile is turned with a ½in (13mm) gouge.

Opposite bottom
The foot is measured to check it will fit the Craft Supplies chuck used when the piece is reversed on to the lathe.

Top right
A fine cut with a skew chisel.

Centre right
A liberal coat of sanding sealer is applied and allowed to dry prior to sanding by . . .

Bottom right
. . . power . . .

Below
. . . and hand.

Above
**The centre is coned
out for future use with
the help of the Stewart
system.**

Opposite
**Once the Stewart has
done its bit all that is
required is a sharp knock.**

Top left
The piece is reversed on to the Craft Supplies chuck.

Centre left
The inside is now gradually removed using a ¼in (6mm) gouge.

Bottom left
As each step is completed it is sanded before moving on.

Opposite top
The thickness is frequently checked using callipers.

Opposite bottom
The finished piece turned to a uniform ¹⁄₁₆in (1.5mm) awaits a coat of oil.

Natural-edge burr elm
(see pages 64–69)
H: 10in (254mm)

Sycamore
D: 11in (279mm)

Natural-edge laburnum
H: 9in (229mm)

Padauk
8in (203mm)

liz and michael o'donnell

After gaining his HND in mechanical engineering, followed by a spell with Hawker Siddeley, Mick decided to fulfil a lifetime ambition by going to sea. Taken on by the Blue Funnel line as a trainee officer, it was on his first deepwater trip to Australia that he realized he had made a mistake. He found the 'them and us – no fraternizing' regime that prevailed between officers and crew hard to accept, and he resigned when the ship docked at Liverpool.

He then joined Rolls-Royce in Derby, working on their nuclear reactor programme. Transferred to Scotland and coming face to face with the reality of nuclear submarines – they'd seemed harmless enough on the drawing board – his conscience eventually got the better of him and, after four years, he quit.

However, Mick and his wife, Liz, had fallen for Scotland and they decided to stay put in their croft. Mick spent his pension on a boat in which he took visitors out on fishing trips. This, plus gardening, crofting, a spell as a lighthouse keeper, and Liz's job as an art teacher, kept the wolf from the door. One of Mick's fishing friends had a lathe and suggested he try his hand at turning. He was hooked! He enrolled for evening classes and bought a Myford, and before long was selling his work to tourists who passed his croft conveniently situated along the coast from John o' Groat's.

In 1981 he headed south, visiting turners whose work he admired – Ray Key, Jim Partridge, the Raffan brothers and the legendary David Pye – an experience which fired him with enthusiasm for his new-found craft. As a founder member of the AWGB, he got together with Ray Key and organized the first Loughborough seminar with visiting turners David Ellsworth and Ed Moulthrop.

Mick met Liz at college and from the start she has always been an integral part of the team. The geometric series, bird shapes and hand colouring are the result of this collaboration. Apart from working with Mick on the turning and helping to run the croft, Liz has a full-time job teaching art in local primary schools.

Mick's engineering background has stood him in good stead. His O'Donnell jaws for the Axminster chuck are to be found in all the best workshops while his recently designed sharpening jig takes the guesswork out of keeping tools sharp – consistently.

Today, Mick divides his time between turning and teaching others the business of turning, and living the life of a crofter. When I referred to their home in Brough in Caithness as the middle of nowhere, Mick replied that he considered it the centre of the universe. He is much in demand as a demonstrator and is a frequent visitor to America and Australia.

Mick might well refer to Brough as the centre of the universe. For my part I felt that after my two-day drive from East Anglia I was in the back of beyond!

Opposite
Selecting a sycamore log from his store exposed to the elements, with Dunnet Head in the distance.

Above
A blank is cut for the end grain of the log.

Centre right
Mounted between centres on a Graduate long-bed lathe, the piece is turned true.

Bottom right
Once it is turned true it is attached to a screw chuck on a Graduate short-bed lathe.

Top
The profile is worked with a bowl gouge and . . .

Above
. . . finished with a scraper ground to a 30° bevel.

Right
The inside is removed using a ¾in (19mm) gouge.

Above
The scraper does the rest.

Left
**Drying the bowl with
a hot-air gun prior to
sanding.**

Left
Power sanding.

Centre
Part of Mick's tool rack.

Bottom
**The piece is reverse mounted
on a jam-fit chuck to the wood-
en jaws of the Axminster, and
the base is then turned off and
rounded.**

Right
A breath of fresh air.

Below
Liz colouring the rim using natural paints and dyes.

Sycamore
(see pages 76–81)
D: 6in (152mm)

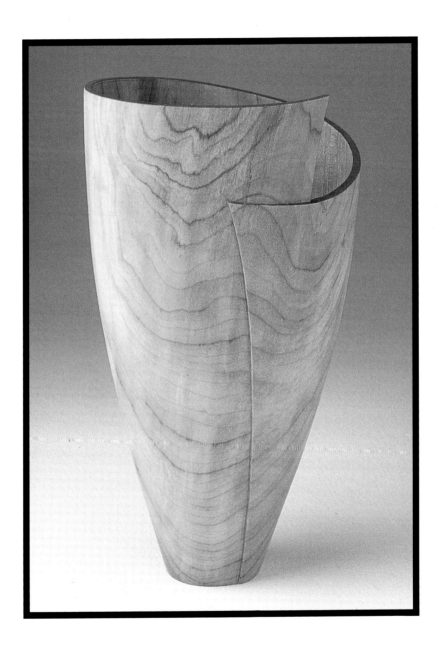

**Sycamore, turned
and carved
H: 12in (305mm)**

**Sycamore hand-
coloured goblets
H: 6in (152mm)**

**Sycamore, hand
coloured
D: 8in (203mm)**

mike scott

Mike Scott returned to England from Australia in 1976, where he had emigrated 11 years previously working in accountancy and administration while bringing up a family. In 1980 a change in direction took him on a journey of self-discovery through the exploration of esoteric disciplines and Eastern philosophy; in the process he acquired the name 'Chai' (which he uses to sign his work), a shortened version of a Sanskrit word given to him by his then Indian guru.

He supported himself during this period through a variety of jobs from building racing cars to vegetarian cookery and general handiwork, before enrolling on a creative arts degree course at Crewe and Alsager College. It was here that he first came across the lathe, little realizing what a seminal moment it was.

He left college after one year and, with the help of the Enterprise Allowance Scheme, set up in business in Warmingham Craft Workshops in Cheshire, initially making carved meditation stools. The purchase of a Coronet Hobby lathe enabled him to expand his range to include a variety of bowls, vases, candlesticks and boxes. These were heady days; the lathe became all-absorbing, with Mike discovering the beauty of wood and what could be made from it. The first eighteen months were touch and go, working all hours and sleeping on the workshop floor, before he moved into the comparative luxury of a £200 on-site caravan.

Devouring all he could read on the subject, it was Dale Nish's excellent *Master Woodturners* that showed him what was possible and encouraged Mike to experiment. A chainsaw was attached to his tool rest for texturing and carving his pieces. In 1986 the purchase of a Gordon Stokes bowl-turning lathe enabled ambitious large-scale work to be produced. Craft fairs gave way to gallery sales with his first one-man show at the Oxford Gallery in 1987.

Increasing demand for his work for exhibitions provided the stimulus to continue to develop and refine his exploration of form and texture. His influences are many – tribal, ethnic, archaeological, architectural, geological and organic. Working predominantly in locally harvested elm and oak burrs, often in a state of degradation, Mike prefers to find an appropriate resolution for each piece when he sees it rather than have a preconceived idea before approaching the lathe. Splits and gaps are repaired with strips of metal and rope found on the beach, while sandblasting, ebonizing and scorching are incorporated to provide contrast to the rich burr grain.

In 1989 he met his future wife, and sternest critic, Hayley Smith. Their distinct contrast of styles has resulted in several successful joint exhibitions. Mike was a founder member of the AWGB and served on the committee for two years. Although no longer a member he acknowledges the contribution the association is making to the development and encouragement of woodturning, and enjoys the camaraderie amongst turners that has resulted from this. He has recently been placed on the Crafts Council Index of Selected Makers.

Mike makes his living solely from the sale of his work through galleries, exhibitions here and abroad, and prestige events such as the Chelsea Crafts Fair. Eric Clapton and Peter Gabriel are among those who collect his work, and the Dalai Lama was presented with a piece as a memento when he visited Wales.

Chai lives and works on Anglesey

in a house previously owned by

fellow turner Jules Tattersall.

Incestous business, woodturning!

Top
**An elm burr is eased on to the
lathe with the help of a pulley.**

Above
**Any loose bark is removed before
starting the lathe.**

Right
**The centre is trued to take the
faceplate using a heavy-duty gouge.**

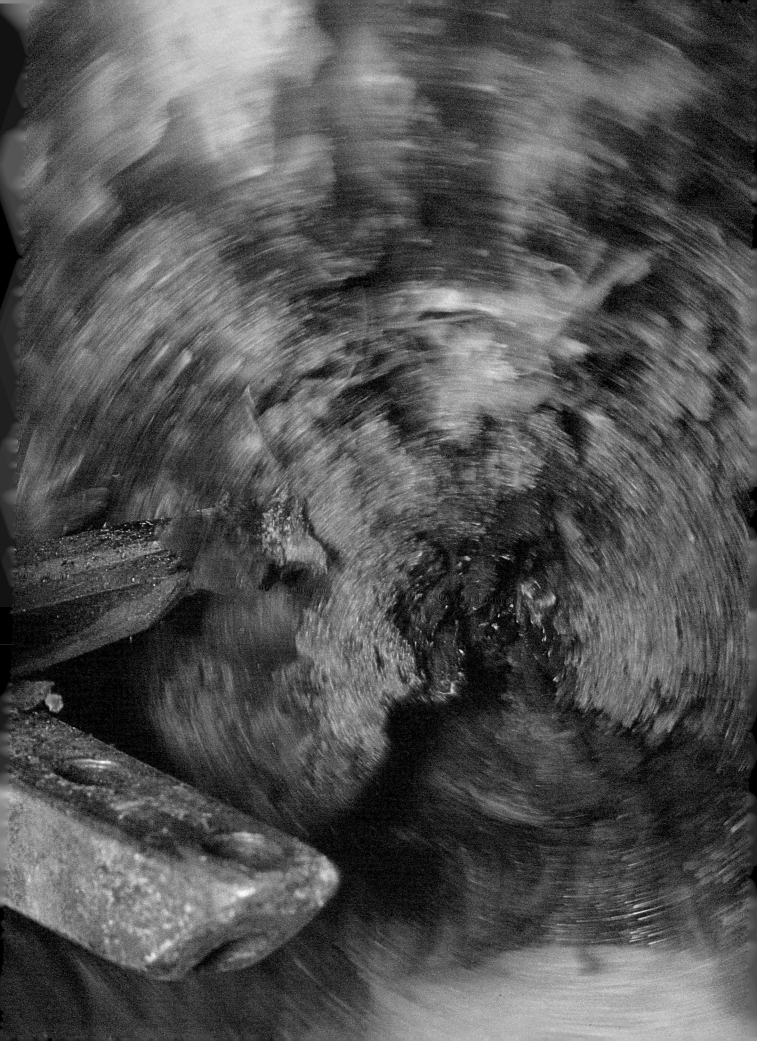

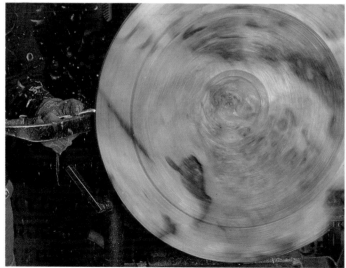

Opposite top
With the burr reversed on to the lathe and held by a faceplate, the inside is removed using a ½in (13mm) gouge.

Opposite bottom
The edge is carefully worked.

Top
With the lathe stationary a chainsaw mounted on a special jig is used to carve initial cuts into the piece.

Centre
By gently rotating the piece in both directions the cut is widened and . . .

Bottom
. . . it is deepened by adjusting the depth screw on the jig.

Right and below
A liberal coat of ebonizing liquid is applied.

The ebonizing is helped by the use of a blow torch.

Below
The finished piece. One of Chai's 'Amphitheatre' series.

**Elm burr, chainsaw
carved and scorched**
(see pages 88–93)
D: 27in (686mm)

Elm burr, sandblasted
D: 14in (356mm)
H: 12in (305mm)

**Elm burr, rim chainsaw
carved and scorched
D: 27in (686mm)**

**Elm, chainsaw carved
and scorched
D: 12in (305mm)
H: 8in (203mm)**

hayley smith

Hayley Smith was born in Wales and from an early age was into art and making things. It comes as no surprise to those who knew her then that she is doing what she does today.

A foundation year at Cardiff Art College was followed by a year studying etching and printmaking in New York, before returning to read for a degree in art education in Cardiff. It was during her second year here that she came across a woodturning lathe for the first time. She formed an immediate rapport with the process and the material, finding new freedom working in three dimensions. Exciting though this period might have been, it was not without its frustrations. The college considered turning to be 'craft' rather than 'art', decent timber was hard to come by, and what tools she was able to lay her hands on were lent on the understanding that she didn't sharpen them too often as this 'wasted the metal'.

In desperation she approached the Arts Council for Wales who put her in touch with Anglesey turner Jules Tattersall, who in turn introduced her to Mike Scott and Don Dennis. Between them they provided her with essential equipment, wood and, above all, moral support. If anything, her experience at college made her even more determined to succeed in her chosen medium.

While still at college she began to make and sell bangles, which helped provide a relatively smooth transition from student to full-time turner, which she became on graduating. Exploration of the bowl/platter form as artifact has replaced the production of bangles, although they still provide bread-and-butter money and are available through Knightsbridge outlets and the Guggenheim Museum Shop in New York.

Today her work is predominantly non-functional. She sees turning as a discipline in which to express herself, accepting what some perceive as its limitations, i.e. the circularity of form. Evident in her current work is the increasing division of the surface into counterbalanced profiles, allowing the grain greater expression while accentuating the circularity.

Working in seasoned native hardwoods, predominantly sycamore, she sees the material as a vehicle of expression rather than an end in itself. This is not to say that she does not value timber – she does passionately – but rather that there is a case to be argued in favour of 'less is more'. Her work is about balance: balance of form, material and what she does with it. Timber is selected with a clear idea of what she intends to create, often with reference to her sketch book which is crammed full of ideas. Strong contemporary forms have classical references, powerful lines are emphasized by areas of subtle contrast, and polished wood surfaces are interspersed by metal and silver wire. Texture is created by finely incised lines, wire brushing or honeycombing with a powered rotating burr, and scorched, blackened areas are enhanced by oil and wax. The form, texture and concentric division of space all strive to achieve a harmony with the wood.

Hayley's work is sold through galleries and exhibitions in the UK, Germany and the USA. She lives on Anglesey with her husband Mike Scott – she got more than she bargained for when she went in search of advice while still at college! Although it would be hard to find two turners producing more contrasting work she values the mutual support they are able to give each other.

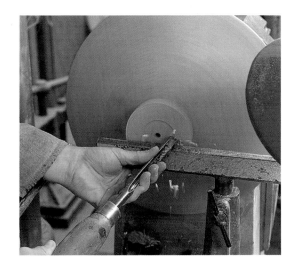

I interviewed Hayley at

Grizedale where she was

artist in residence during

the summer of 1994,

following in the footsteps

of the likes of Merryll Saylan,

Maurice Mullins and

Jim Partridge.

Opposite
Sharp tools are essential for the fine work that Hayley does.

Top left
Truing the foot. This is turned from a waste piece of sycamore glued to the base of the blank in order to save wood.

Top right
Knots etc. are filled with superglue.

Above left
The profile is worked with a ½in (13mm) gouge and . . .

Above right
. . . is finished by power sanding.

Right
To eliminate any chance of movement the piece is superglued to a Craft Supplies chuck.

Below
The inside is worked with a ½in (13mm) gouge.

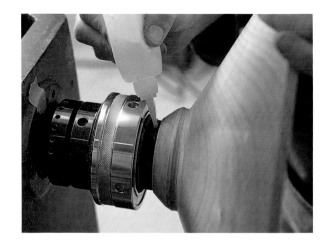

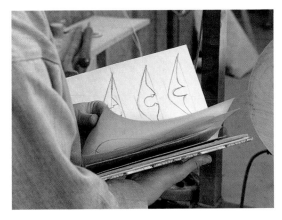

Left
The sketch book is frequently referred to.

Below
A ring is detailed using a parting tool.

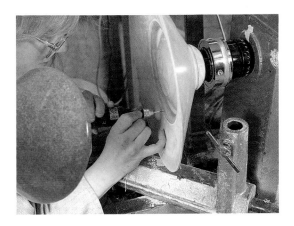

Left
A mini-electric tool is used to drill small holes which will be filled with silver wire.

Left, top, centre and bottom
**Excess wire is trimmed
off using wire cutters
and a parting tool.**

Opposite top
**A blow torch is used to
ebonize the central ring.**

Opposite bottom
**The finished piece awaits
its final polish.**

Sycamore
D: 14in (356mm)

Sycamore
D: 15in (381mm)

Ash
D: 8in (203mm)
H: 8in (203mm)

Sycamore
D: 14in (356mm)

jules tattersall

Jules Tattersall was born in Cheshire and, apart from a brief spell in the Caribbean where his father ran a yacht charter business, was brought up on Anglesey. Summer holidays were spent working as a barman on the Irish Sea ferries saving up to pay for flying lessons. Eventually he fulfilled a lifetime ambition by qualifying as a pilot. University followed and it was in his final year reading for a degree in Social Geography that he was head-hunted by Bristow to train as a helicopter pilot. Unfortunately, due to the common problem of making the transition from fixed wing to rotary, he failed to qualify. Rather than face the ignominy of family and friends he 'fled in shame' to New Zealand, and after three months picking apples there, he moved to Australia where he ended up working in a boat yard in Sydney.

It was the simple beauty of a Richard Raffan bowl which caught his eye in a Sydney gallery that made Jules decide to try his hand at woodturning and he enrolled in a trade course at Sydney Technical College. He supported himself by doing washing up jobs at night, while turning by day, and was soon selling pieces through craft fairs and galleries. His first contract was with the National Trust for 300 needle cases in huon pine.

Jules readily admits to being influenced by the quality and style of Australian turners, in particular by the expatriate Richard Raffan who generously invited him to his workshop to watch and learn. To this day he shares Raffan's pragmatic semi-production approach to the business. Despite his success Jules has managed to keep his feet firmly on the ground and claims to be just as happy turning a run of banskia vases as producing individual pieces for galleries.

In 1987 he returned to Anglesey where his family still lived and property was cheap. Here, from his workshop perched on a rock overlooking the sea, using a few basic tools on a somewhat beaten-up Poole Wood lathe, he produces a variety of hollow forms and bowls, whose feel and balance are both stimulating and soothing. He uses a variety of local hardwoods from managed sources plus the odd container-load of burrs from Down Under. When he's not at his lathe he enjoys taking bracing walks along Anglesey's coastline.

Jules admires all turners who can make a living from their work, and is well aware that the need to survive often leads to compromise. The level of creativity aspired to is often inhibited by the pressure to produce popular work that suits the public's notoriously conservative tastes. Apart from the early influence of Richard Raffan and the sheer beauty of David Ellsworth's work, most of his influences are subtle. He feels that the greatest challenge turners face today is to avoid being overtly influenced by other turners while at the same time keeping an eye on what they are up to. 'The integrity of our originality depends on how we control these plagiaristic urges, and mould them into something we can be proud to truthfully call our own'. This is not as easy as it sounds. After all, how many ways are there of turning a banskia nut?

Jules sells his work through galleries and prestigious outlets throughout the UK as well as at the Guggenheim Museum Shop in New York. He also drives thousands of miles each year attending craft fairs, as he enjoys meeting the public – and needs their money! He has no desire for his work to become particularly exclusive, but rather strives to improve the quality while keeping it affordable to the public at large.

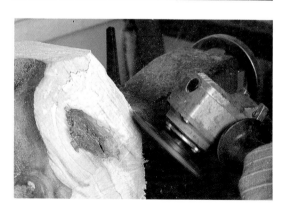

It was blowing such a gale when I visited Jules on Anglesey that at any moment I expected his wooden shed of a workshop to become airborne. No need for dust extraction here – just open a couple of windows!

Opposite top
Mounting the block between centres on the Poole Wood lathe.

Opposite centre
Rough shaping the blank with a chainsaw and . . .

Opposite bottom
. . . with an angle grinder fitted with a superthin blade.

Top right
Initial cuts are made with a ½in (13mm) deep fluted gouge.

Top centre
Shearing cuts shape the profile with a foot turned to reverse fit into the jaws of the Axminster chuck.

Below
The profile is fine tuned.

Below right
The surface is etched by working the superthin blade against the turning piece.

Above
The desired effect is
achieved.

Right
Wire brushing to achieve
a textured finish.

Top left
A liberal coating of Danish oil is applied.

Centre left
Buffing.

Below
Using a clothes peg to mark the desired depth, the core is removed by an auger.

Opposite
There is only one way to remove the shavings: take the piece off the lathe and give it a good shake.

Right
The centre is hollowed using the Stewart system.

Below
The thickness of the wall is frequently checked with callipers.

Left
With the piece reversed onto a jam-fit chuck, the foot is turned off and blended into the rest of the body using the superthin blade.

117

Ash
(see pages 112–117)
H: 10in (254mm)

Red gum burr
D: 12in (305mm)

Ebonized burr elm
D: 14in (356mm)

Xanthorea
H: 12in (305mm)

don white

I was having a meal with Paul Clare and his wife when Paul passed me the salad bowl and asked me what I thought of it. I must have replied that it was a very nice piece or words to that effect. 'Nice!' he exploded. 'What do you mean nice? It's bloody beautiful – you will not come across a better example of domestic turning anywhere.' I looked underneath and had my suspicions confirmed. It was the work of Don White.

I tracked Don down to his workshop in a converted cow shed outside Bath. Of all the workshops I have visited in my travels his has to be the most organized. Everything from blanks to tools have their place. Two industrial-size extractors remove all trace of dust and shavings. This is the workshop of a serious woodturner.

Don was brought up in the Cotswolds. On leaving school he joined a firm of shop fitters who taught him everything from carpentry to wiring. During a lull in business a friend told him that there was work around for drivers with their own trucks. He went ahead and bought one and set up in the light haulage business. Like most self-employed people he found that work could be spasmodic and it was while looking around for something to fill the time between jobs that he came across Frank Pain's book on woodturning. He decided to give it a try and advertised locally for a second-hand lathe. His only reply was from a Harry Baker who, although he didn't have a lathe to sell, said that Don was welcome to have a go on his Myford. Don was, and still is, mesmerized by the process. Harry lent him a lathe attachment to run off an electric drill. It was after burning out three motors in a week that Don decided the time had come to buy his own lathe. The family car was sold and a Coronet Major installed in the garage. Don was soon producing the usual range of craft shop items. His truck driving enabled him to visit outlets around the country and supply them on a sale-or-return basis.

It was after attending the Parnham House seminar in 1980 where he listened to and watched the likes of Ellsworth, Stocksdale, Raffan and Key that he decided to concentrate on turning and employ someone else to drive the truck. Before long he decided to get rid of the truck altogether. He moved out of the garage and set up shop for a while in an old school house before moving to his present workshop.

Don regards himself as a jobbing turner and will tackle anything within the capacity of his lathe and ability. Since 1980 the 'humble salad bowl' has been the mainstay of his work. His individual pieces are sold through selected galleries and exhibitions organized by the Gloucestershire Guild of Craftsmen of which he is an active member.

What with no phone and no signpost,
Don took some tracking down before I
found him in his farmyard workshop
at the end of a long drive a few miles
outside Bath. It was well worth the effort.

Top right
**A 6in (152mm) faceplate
is attached to an ash blank.**

Centre right
**A weight is also attached
to compensate for the
uneven balance.**

Below
**Working on the profile
with a ½in (13mm) gouge
on a Graduate lathe.**

**Coning out the centre
using the Stewart system.**

**Removing the centre using
a ½in (13mm) gouge.**

Below
**Although the trend is to
conceal chuck marks Don
is quite happy to make a
feature of his. The added
advantage is that they
can be returned to the
lathe in the future for
repolishing.**

Bottom
**When you've turned as
many bowls as Don has
you don't need callipers
to check the thickness.**

Right
The workshop.

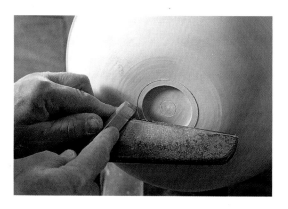

Top left and centre
Power and hand sensing.

Below left
**The finished bowl is
treated with corn oil.**

Right
**The workshop showing
neatly stacked blanks**

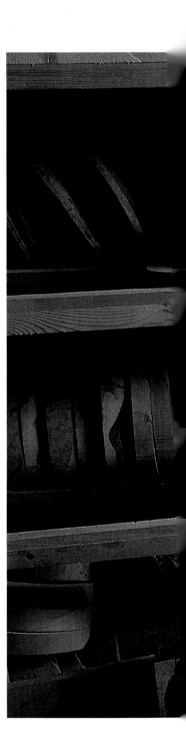

Ash bowls
D: 6–18in
(152–457mm)

**Burr elm, turned
and carved
D: 15in (381mm)**

Burr elm
D: 18in (457mm)

Birch-masur
D: 6in (152mm)

david woodward

The miners' strike of 1974 affected us all in different ways – remember the three day week? – but Arthur Scargill is probably unaware of the crucial part he played in the career of David Woodward, woodturner. In those days he was working as a forester in the Forest of Dean supplying the coal industry with timber for pit props and blocks. He had gone into forestry after completing a foundation year at Newport College of Art. Listening with interest to stories the old timers told of woodland crafts such as bodging led to experiments with a pole lathe. This was soon replaced by a Black & Decker and this in turn by a Tyme Avon. The aforementioned strike saw to it that what started out as a hobby soon became his only source of income.

Initially he worked from home, selling at craft fairs, before moving into a purpose-built workshop and gallery in a craft centre in the book town of Hay-on-Wye. From here he produces a range of bowls and platters in local hardwoods – especially burrs – from managed sources. Visitors to the gallery are able to watch him at work through a glass partition and are occasionally so taken with the process that they end up buying the piece straight off the lathe.

His years spent working in forestry have given David an unrivalled knowledge of wood and where to find the very best examples. He is happy to share this with others, and it was by supplying the likes of Don White in the early days that his eyes were opened to what was achievable in turning. He recently came across a particularly fine example of burr elm and, deciding that the huge burr was just too stunning to keep to himself, shared it with Don and Bert Marsh. I can't think of many turners who would be so generous!

Although David rates and acknowledges the influence of the likes of Don and Bert, he feels there is also a lot to be learned from turners of a bygone age and he is a frequent visitor to rural craft museums. The treen rescued from the Mary Rose is a case in point.

He is a dab hand with the chainsaw, frequently demonstrating at seminars on its safe use – an aspect all too often overlooked by turners. He feels passionately about what is happening to our woodland and thinks we should pay more attention to the destruction going on on our own doorstep before we start worrying about the Amazon rainforest. When not at the lathe he goes fishing. Whereas other turners might have photographs of their work on the workshop wall, David's are more likely to show his latest record catch.

David's set up must be the envy of most turners. A large light workshop with gallery attached, in the middle of a busy craft complex in Hay-on-Wye. No shortage of customers here.

Opposite top
Shaping the elm burr into a rough cylinder on the bandsaw.

Opposite bottom
Removing loose bark with a screwdriver.

Left
The piece is attached to the Graduate lathe by a home-made screw chuck made from a coach bolt with wooden washers used to adjust the depth.

Above
The exterior is worked with a ½in (13mm) gouge and a recess turned to fit the O'Donnell 2in (50mm) jaws of his Axminster chuck.

Left
A visitor to the gallery watches the piece take shape.

Below
The only way to check the shape is to take the piece off the lathe and stand it on its end.

Bottom
Back on the lathe for fine tuning with a ¼in (6mm) gouge.

Right
Applying sanding sealer.

Top left and right
Wet/dry sanding.

Above left
With the piece reversed onto the lathe, the centre is removed using a ½in (13mm) gouge.

Above right
A bead is detailed with a 1/4in (6mm) gouge.

Opposite top
Sanding by hand is preferred to power sanding, working through from 120 to 400 grit.

Opposite bottom
The finished piece on the lathe.

Burr elm
(see pages 136–141)
D: 10in (254mm)

Yew
D: 8in (203mm)

Yew
D: 12in (305mm)

Burr elm
D: 14in (356mm)

About the Author

Tony Boase is a professional photographer specializing in fashion and advertising. Away from the cameras he indulges himself in his lifetime obsession of woodturning, finding the hours spent on his Graduate lathe a perfect antidote to the stress (see above) of coping with the English climate and temperamental models. He lives in East Anglia with his wife, Jacky, a photographic stylist, and their two children, Petra and Marc, by whom he is referred to as 'Turning Mad'.

Titles available from GMC Publications

Books

Woodworking Plans and Projects GMC Publications

40 More Woodworking Plans and Projects GMC Publications

Woodworking Crafts Annual GMC Publications

Woodworkers' Career and Educational Source Book
   GMC Publications

Woodworkers' Courses & Source Book GMC Publications

Woodturning Techniques GMC Publications

Useful Woodturning Projects GMC Publications

Green Woodwork Mike Abbott

Easy to Make Dolls' House Accessories Andrea Barham

Making Little Boxes from Wood John Bennett

Woodturning Masterclass Tony Boase

Furniture Restoration and Repair for Beginners
   Kevin Jan Bonner

Woodturning Jewellery Hilary Bowen

The Incredible Router Jeremy Broun

Electric Woodwork Jeremy Broun

Woodcarving: A Complete Course Ron Butterfield

Making Fine Furniture: Projects Tom Darby

Restoring Rocking Horses Clive Green & Anthony Dew

Heraldic Miniature Knights Peter Greenhill

Make Your Own Dolls' House Furniture Maurice Harper

Practical Crafts: Seat Weaving Ricky Holdstock

Multi-centre Woodturning Ray Hopper

Complete Woodfinishing Ian Hosker

Practical Crafts: Woodfinishing Handbook Ian Hosker

Woodturning: A Source Book of Shapes John Hunnex

Making Shaker Furniture Barry Jackson

Upholstery: A Complete Course David James

Upholstery Techniques and Projects David James

The Upholsterer's Pocket Reference Book David James

Designing and Making Wooden Toys Terry Kelly

Making Dolls' House Furniture Patricia King

Making Victorian Dolls' House Furniture Patricia King

Making and Modifying Woodworking Tools Jim Kingshott

The Workshop Jim Kingshott

Sharpening: The Complete Guide Jim Kingshott

Turning Wooden Toys Terry Lawrence

Making Board, Peg and Dice Games Jeff & Jennie Loader

Making Wooden Toys and Games Jeff & Jennie Loader

Bert Marsh: Woodturner Bert Marsh

The Complete Dolls' House Book Jean Nisbett

The Secrets of the Dolls' House Makers Jean Nisbett

Wildfowl Carving, Volume 1 Jim Pearce

Make Money from Woodturning Ann & Bob Phillips

Guide to Marketing Jack Pigden

Woodcarving Tools, Materials and Equipment Chris Pye

Carving on Turning Chris Pye

Making Tudor Dolls' Houses Derek Rowbottom

Making Georgian Dolls' Houses Derek Rowbottom

Making Period Dolls' House Furniture
   Derek & Sheila Rowbottom

Woodturning: A Foundation Course Keith Rowley

Turning Miniatures in Wood John Sainsbury

Pleasure and Profit from Woodturning Reg Sherwin

Making Unusual Miniatures Graham Spalding

Woodturning Wizardry David Springett

Adventures in Woodturning David Springett

Furniture Projects Rod Wales

Decorative Woodcarving Jeremy Williams

Videos

Dennis White Teaches Woodturning

        Part 1 Turning Between Centres

        Part 2 Turning Bowls

        Part 3 Boxes, Goblets and Screw Threads

        Part 4 Novelties and Projects

        Part 5 Classic Profiles

        Part 6 Twists and Advanced Turning

John Jordan Bowl Turning

John Jordan Hollow Turning

Jim Kingshott Sharpening the Professional Way

Jim Kingshott Sharpening Turning and Carving Tools

Ray Gonzalez Carving a Figure: The Female Form

David James The Traditional Upholstery Workshop

        Part I: Drop-in and Pinstuffed Seats

David James The Traditional Upholstery Workshop

        Part II: Stuffover Upholstery

GMC Publications regularly produces new books and videos on a wide range of woodworking and craft subjects, and an increasing number of specialist magazines, all available on subscription:

Magazines

WOODTURNING   WOODCARVING   BUSINESSMATTERS

All these publications are available through bookshops and newsagents, or may be ordered by post from the publishers at:
166 High Street, Lewes, East Sussex BN7 1XU
Telephone (01273) 477374, Fax (01273) 478606

Credit card orders are accepted

PLEASE WRITE OR PHONE FOR A FREE CATALOGUE